**Northwick Park
Primary Academy**

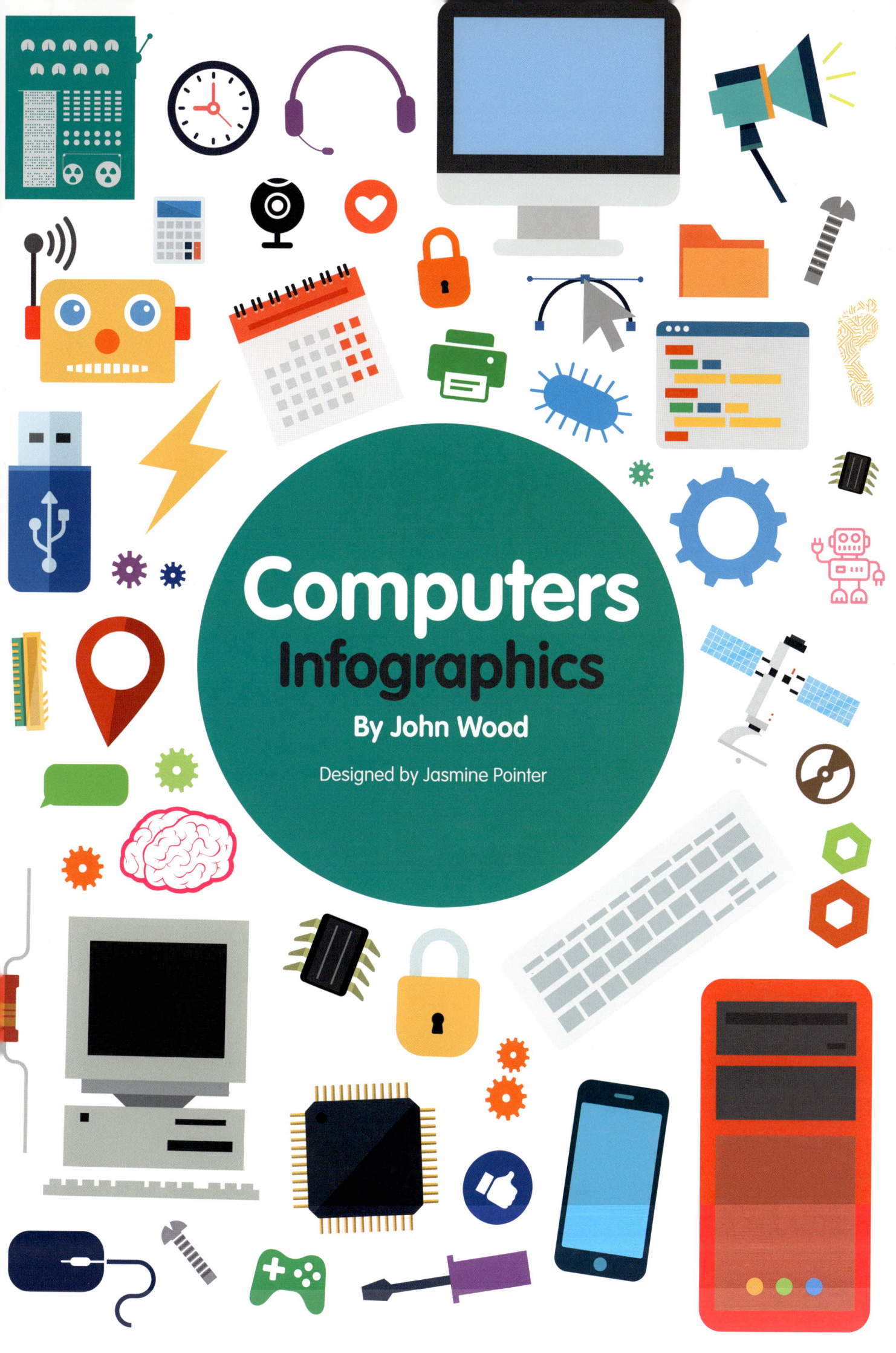

BookLife PUBLISHING

©2018
BookLife Publishing
King's Lynn
Norfolk, PE30 4LS

ISBN: 978-1-78637-413-4

Written by:
John Wood

Edited by:
Kirsty Holmes

Designed by:
Jasmine Pointer

A catalogue record for this book is available from the British Library.

All facts, statistics, web addresses and URLs in this book were verified as valid and accurate at time of writing. No responsibility for any changes to external websites or references can be accepted by either the author or publisher.

All rights reserved. Printed in Malaysia.

Photo Credits

2 – legrandshow. 3 – Lightkite. 4 – ShadeDesign, gst, ArtAlex, LuckyDesigner, flower travelin' man. 5 – vectorpocket, Tierre3012, FoxyImage, maglyvi. 6 – Abscent, Be Panya, ByEmo. 7 – VectorShow, legrandshow. 8 – Abscent, ShadeDesign, jkcDesign, Red monkey. 9 – Reenya, Panimoni, Fouaddesigns, Iurii Kiliian, Incomible. 10 – MircoOne, Iconic Bestiary, Jane Kelly, chuhastock. 11 – AlexHliv, Rachael Arnot, venimo. 12 – Julia Tim, CW craftsman, flower travelin' man, Titov Nikolai. 13 – RoryDesign, Maxim Rumyantsev, Sentavio. 14 – Lisa Kolbasa, Victor Z, hanss. 15 – KittyVector, Kit8.net. 16 – Hilch, BreezyInt, Sulee_R, Dinosoft Labs, robuart, Nadia Snopek, Jesus Sanz. 17 – Petrovic Igor, Ico Maker, monicaodo. 18 – phipatbig, Artem Mashchenko, Sentavio, Sirin_bird, shuvector, Igrapop. 19 – Art Alex, VectorSun, Sudowoodo. 20 – MikeStyle, Perfect Vectors, robuart, lukpedclub, Macrovector. 21 – Fouaddesigns, Andy Frith, didiaCC, Gaidamashchuk. 22 – Aniwhite, Ciripasca, Pranch. 23 – Trifonenkolvan, Yaroslav Okhranchuk, Bonezboyz, Aurora72. 24 – Kit8.net, Antun Hirsman, Oceloti, Vikation. 25 – wild wind, Kit8.net, Makc, Sunflowerr, tovovan. 26 – Vanatchanan, Bloomicon, Good_Stock. 27 – BigMouse, Fullvector, Kit8.net. 28 – Golden Sikorka, Kaleo, Jemastock. 29 – Andrew Rybalko, July Pluto. 30 – Jesus Sanz, ProStockStudio, Graphic.mooi.

Images are courtesy of Shutterstock.com. With thanks to Getty Images, Thinkstock Photo and iStockphoto.

Computers
Infographics

Contents

Page 4 What Is a Computer?
Page 6 Digital Language
Page 8 Hardware
Page 10 Software
Page 12 Smartphones
Page 14 The Internet
Page 16 Computers in Everything
Page 18 Rise of the Computers
Page 20 Smaller Stuff
Page 22 AI
Page 25 Extreme Computers
Page 26 Supercomputers
Page 28 Future Devices
Page 30 Activity
Page 31 Glossary
Page 32 Index

Words that look like this are explained in the glossary on page 31.

What Is a Computer?

A computer is a machine that is really, really good at following instructions. The part of a computer that sorts through instructions, called a central processing unit (CPU), can carry out between 1 and 3 <u>billion</u> instructions per second, depending on how powerful the CPU is.

1–3 Billion Instructions per Second

Types of Computer

Desktops are big and plugged into sockets, so they can't move around. Inside a computer are all the things it needs to work, like the CPU. This is all inside the desktop. Laptops are smaller. They have batteries, and can be used anywhere. Tablets and smartphones are very small so they can easily be carried around. The batteries and computer are behind the screen.

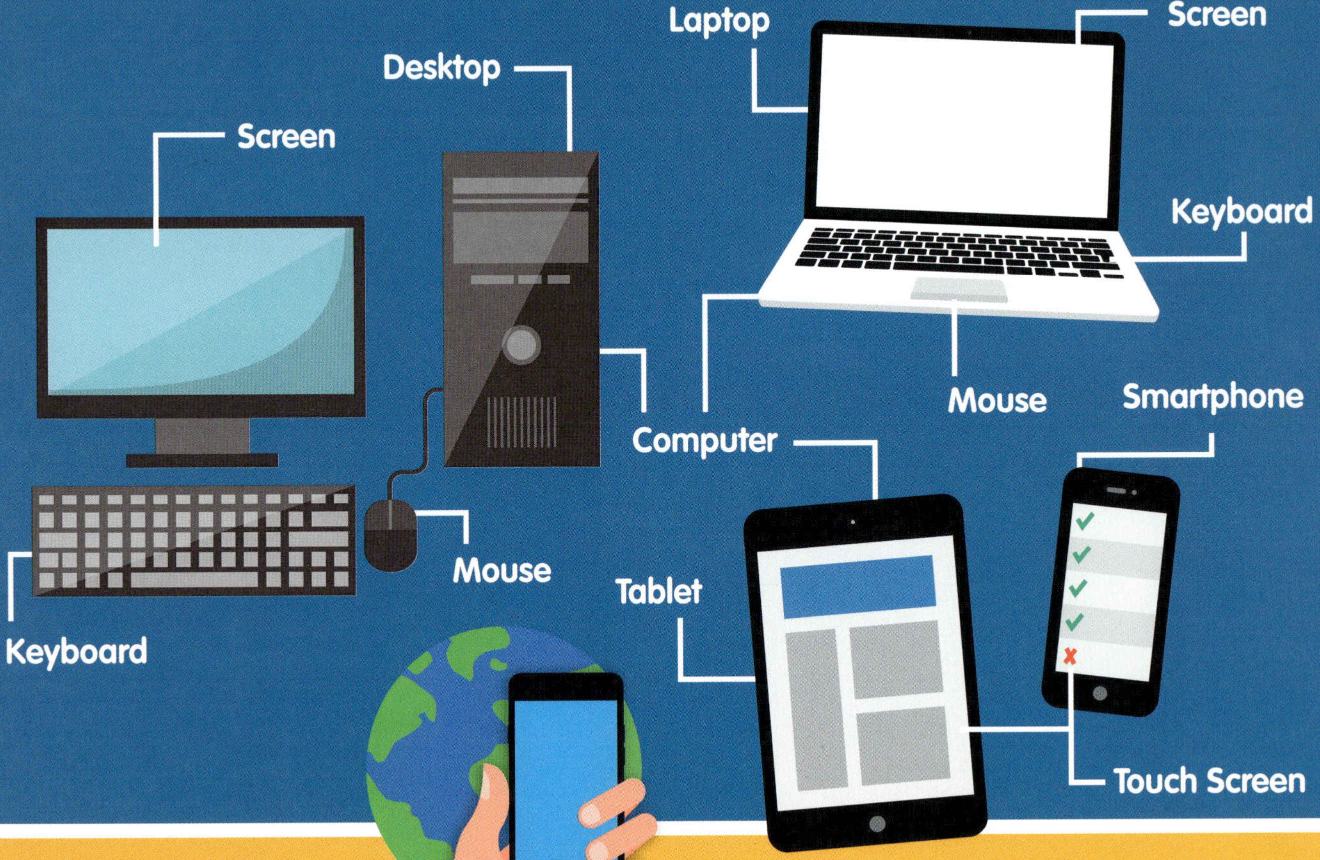

Most of the desktops that people use are called PCs (Personal Computers). There are between 1.4 and 2 billion PCs used all over the world.

In 2020, more than half of people in the world will probably have a smartphone.

Computers are everywhere. Even things like cars, traffic lights and street lamps can have computers inside them. Many appliances, like fridges, washing machines and TVs can also be fitted with a computer. This is sometimes called smart technology. For example, smart TVs are TVs with computers inside. A fridge with a computer in it would be called a smart fridge.

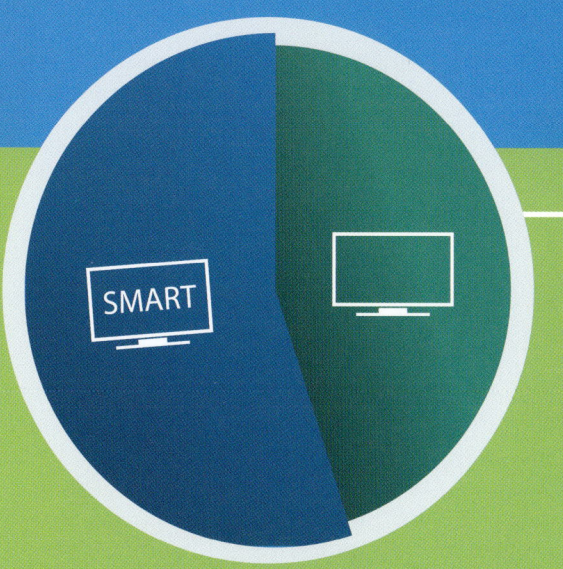

More than half of TVs sold in 2017 were smart TVs.

Schools use computers to help teachers teach and children learn. However, there are also computers which are used to hold lots of information. Keeping track of information about teachers, pupils and lessons can help the school to run smoothly.

In recent years, almost half the schools without computers in the classroom have said they will soon start using them. This means many more schools will have tablets in the future.

In the UK, almost 70% of schools use tablet computers in the classroom.

Digital Language

Digital Computer Checklist

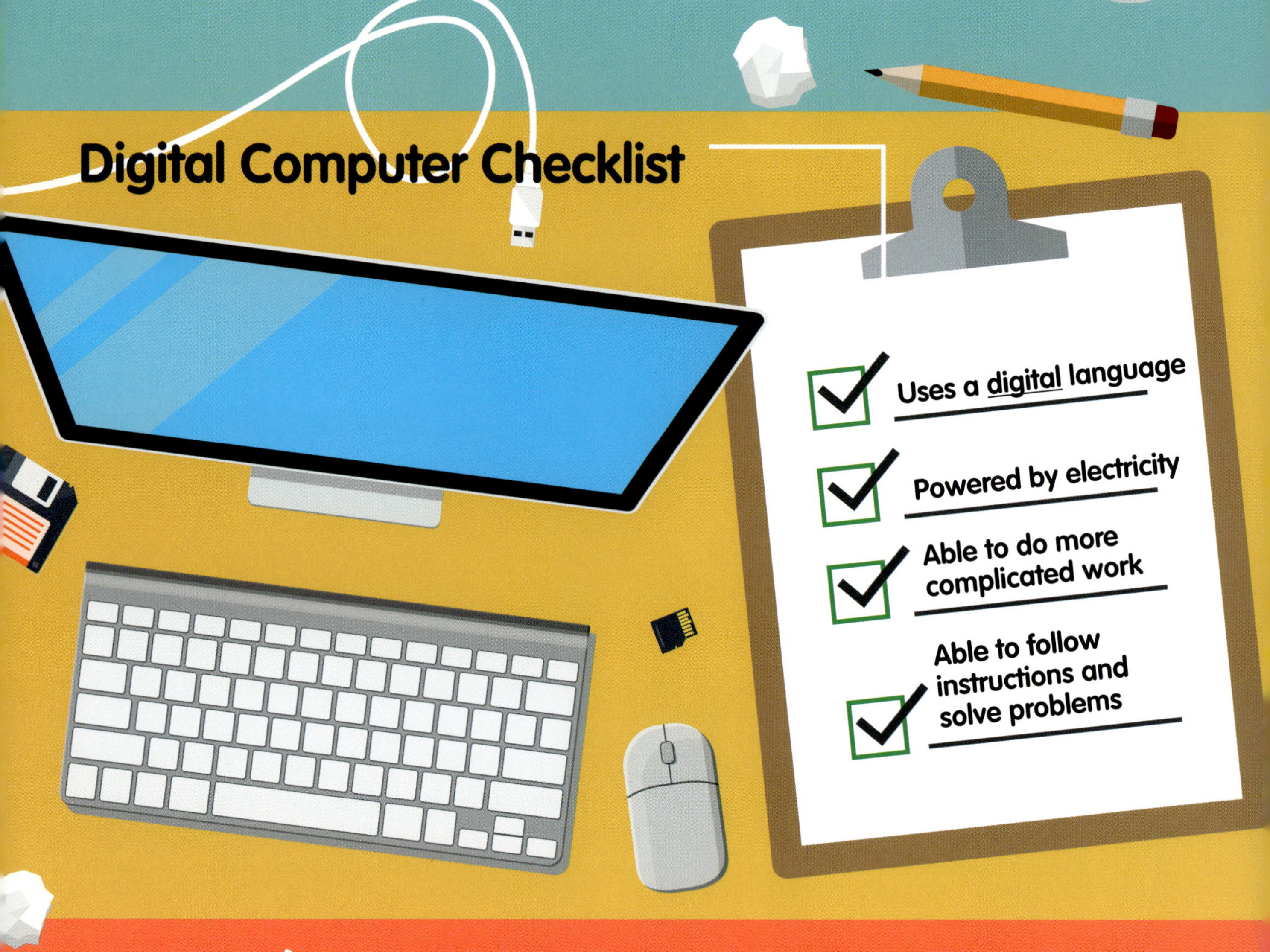

- ✓ Uses a <u>digital language</u>
- ✓ Powered by electricity
- ✓ Able to do more complicated work
- ✓ Able to follow instructions and solve problems

How Does Digital Language Work?

When a button is pressed on a computer's keyboard or screen, electrical <u>signals</u> are sent to a <u>microchip</u>. There are two different electronic signals – off and on. Off means 0, and on means 1. This is called binary language, and it is the language that computers use. Everything a computer does is controlled by these 1's and 0's.

The microchip is made up of transistors. Transistors are like tiny electronic switches. The 1's turn a transistor on, while the 0's keep it off. The pattern of transistors which are turned on and off (or the pattern of 1's and 0's) are the instructions for the computer.

Counting to 10 in Binary

Below are the numbers 0–10, and next to them is what those numbers look like in binary code.

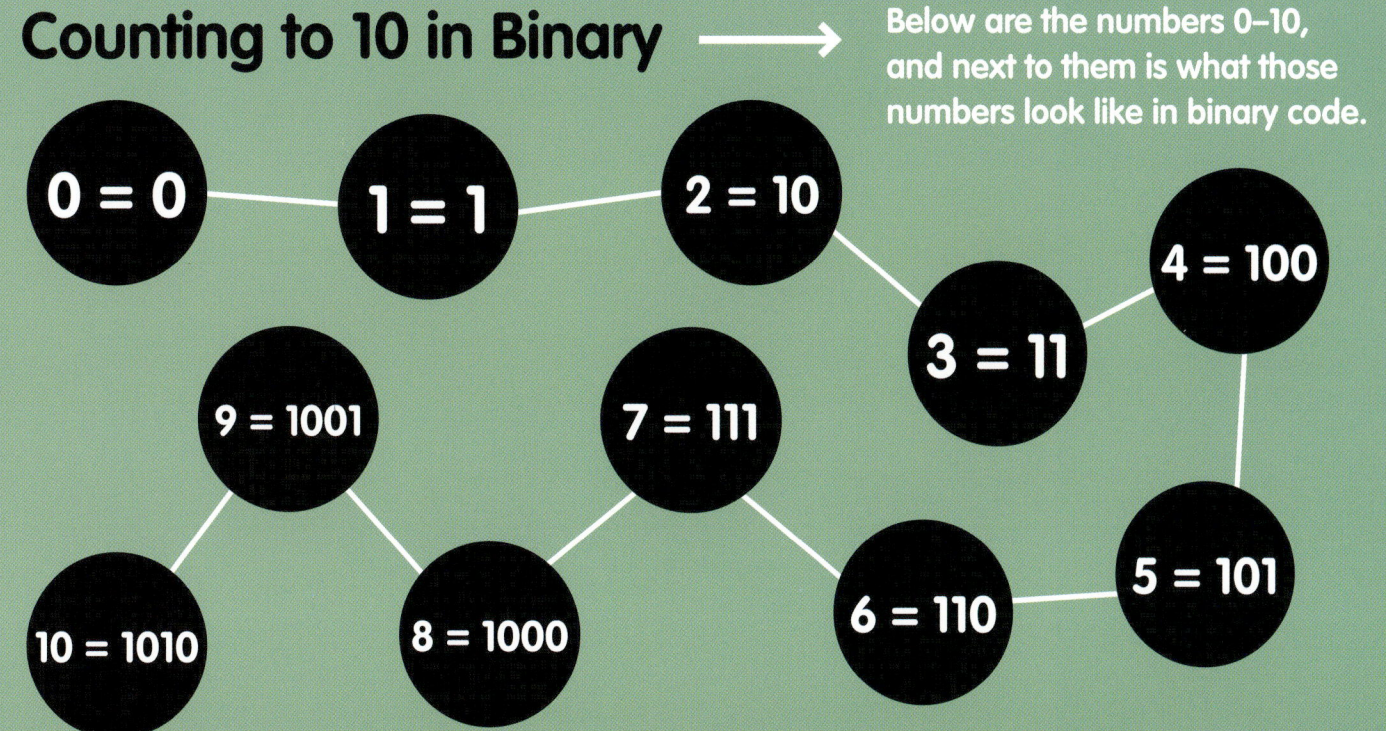

0 = 0
1 = 1
2 = 10
3 = 11
4 = 100
5 = 101
6 = 110
7 = 111
8 = 1000
9 = 1001
10 = 1010

History of Computers

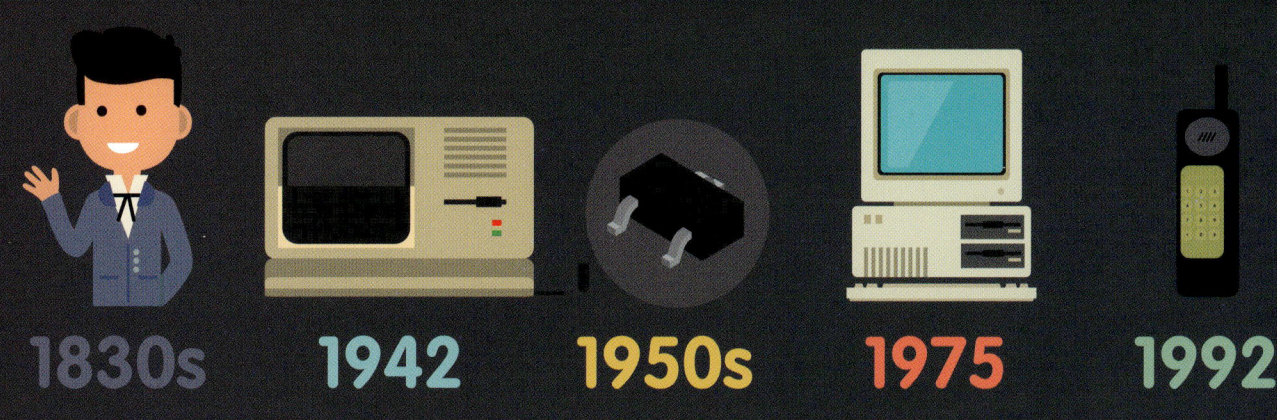

1830s — Charles Babbage had an idea for an 'analytical engine'. This machine was not powered by electricity, but it could do maths like a giant calculator. Many people think of this as the first idea for a computer.

1942 — The first ever electric digital computer was built in 1942. It was made by John Vincent Atanasoff and his assistant, Clifford E Berry. It was called the Atanasoff-Berry Computer, or ABC for short.

1950s — New types of digital computers were built, which used transistors.

1975 — The first PC, the MITS Altair 8800, was invented. This was the first computer meant for people to use in their homes.

1992 — The first smartphone, the IBM Simon, was invented. It had a touchscreen, could send emails, and had a built-in calendar, notepad and clock.

Hardware

Hardware means the physical parts of a computer. This includes the things outside the computer, like the mouse, keyboard and screen, as well as all the tiny electrical components inside the computer, like the CPU, memory and the power supply.

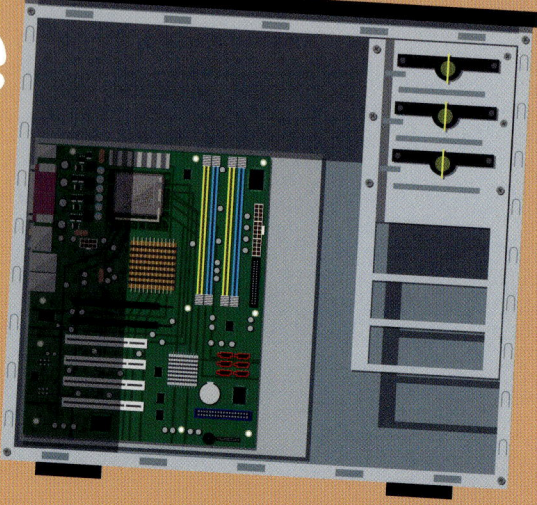

Many desktops have more than one CPU. Dual-core computers have two CPUs, and quad-core computers have four. Octa-core computers have eight. The more processors there are, the more powerful the computer will be.

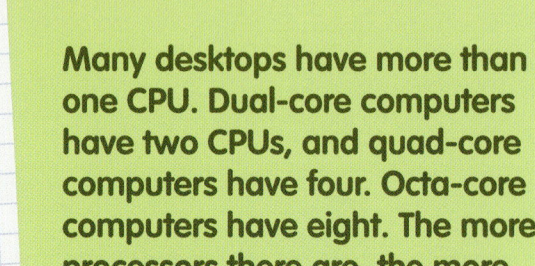
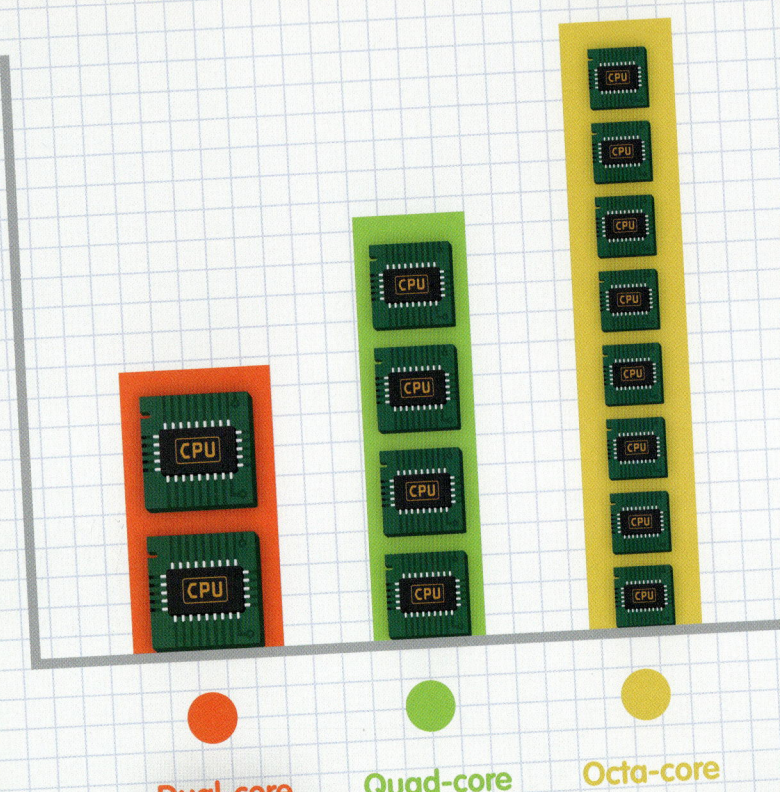

- Dual-core
- Quad-core
- Octa-core

unsafe
60°C
safe

CPUs can get very hot. That is why the inside of a computer also has fans inside, to cool down the hardware.

The CPU of a computer is kept below 60°C by the fans to stop any damage. Without the fans, the inside of a computer would get much hotter.

The motherboard is the main board. It is full of circuits, and links all the different hardware together. All the components and parts of a computer are connected to the motherboard.

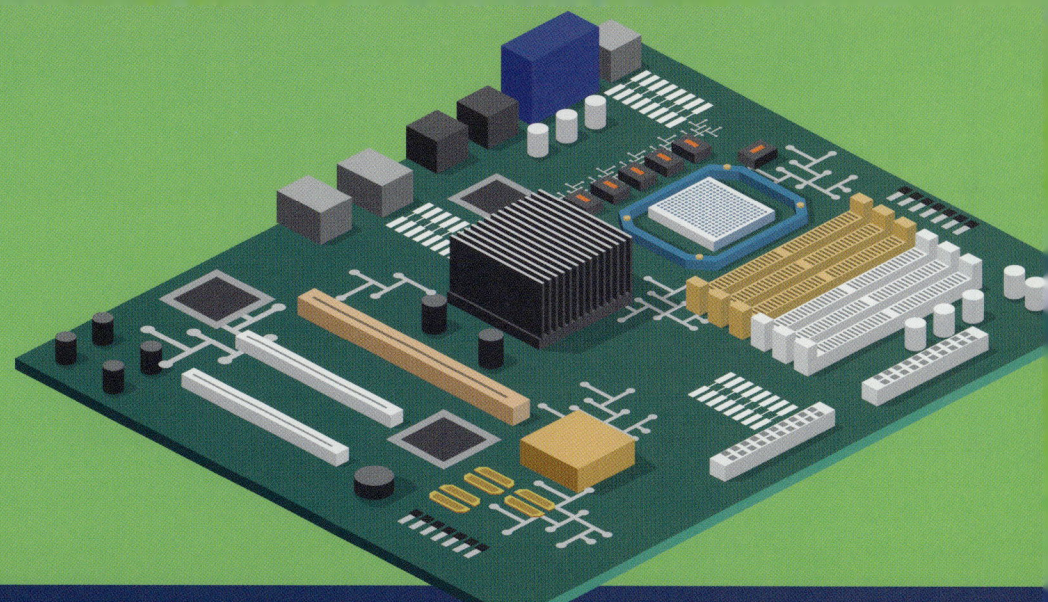

A computer has two different kinds of memory. Random access memory (RAM) is a component used by the CPU to store information that it is processing for a short amount of time. The hard drive is a component that stores memory forever, or until that memory is deleted.

Many computers nowadays have 1 terabyte (TB) of space on the hard drive. This is enough to store 17,000 hours of music.

The largest hard drive ever made was 60 TB – the people at Google have worked out that this might be big enough to store every book that's ever been published.

In 2010, the people at Google estimated that there had been 129,864,880 books published.

Software

Software is not like the physical parts of a computer. You can't touch it. Instead, software is the instructions a computer uses to know how to do things like writing, drawing or accessing the internet.

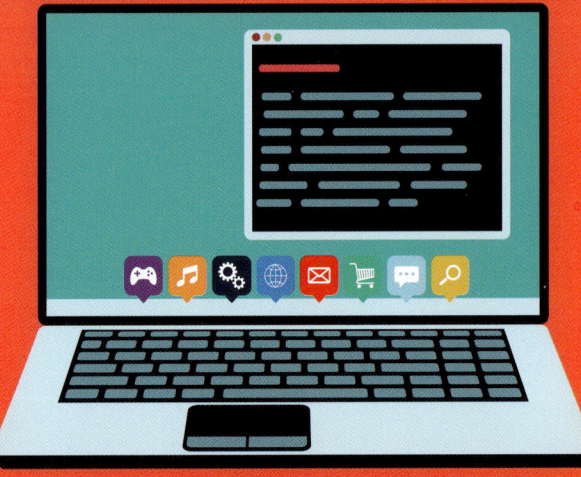

Programs are written by computer programmers. The computer programmers write out instructions for the computer in code. This is called coding. There are hundreds of different coding languages that programmers use.

Different languages are better at different jobs.

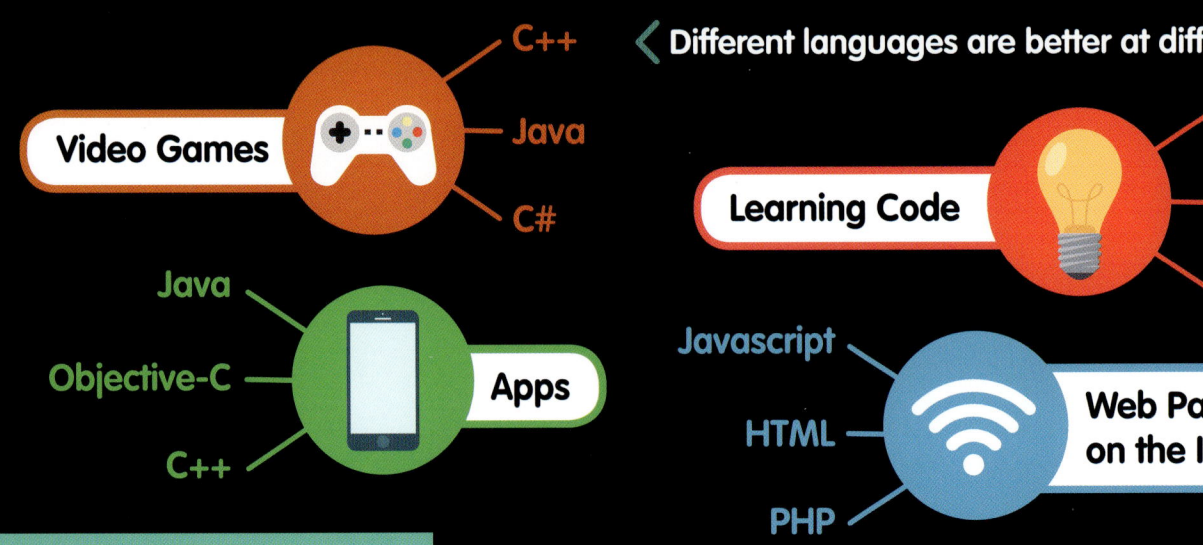

YouTube was written in a language called Python.

Computers translate coding languages into binary. Some coding languages are high-level and others are low-level. The lower the level of the language, the more like binary code it is. Higher level languages are usually easier for humans to write.

Java is the most popular coding language.

Here are some different types of coding languages, from high to low-level.

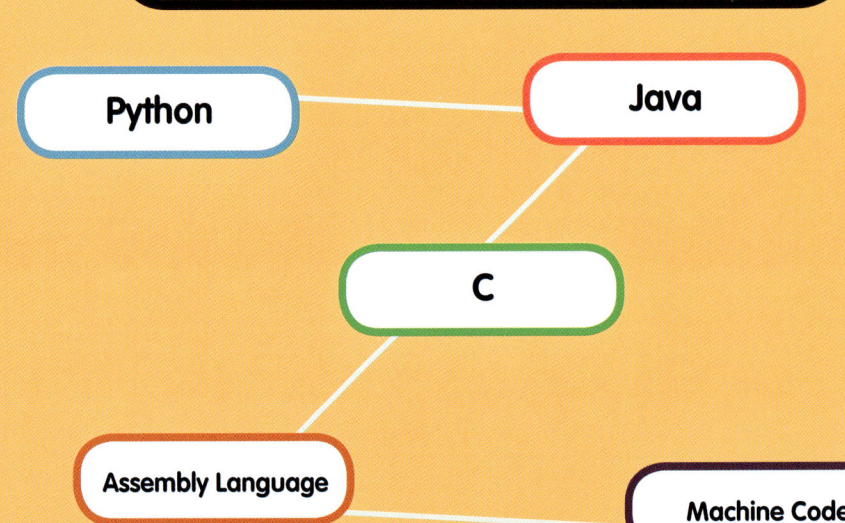

Some programs are written by one programmer, whereas others are made by hundreds and hundreds of programmers. For example, Google employed 18,593 computer programmers in 2014. Lots of programmers will work on each bit of Google's software.

The reason that Google's homepage is so blank is because the people who created it, Sergey Brin and Larry Page, weren't very good at coding in HTML. They could only make a simple page, but decided to keep it.

There are around 20 million programmers in the world. Most of these are in the US and India. India has a very fast-growing number of computer programmers.

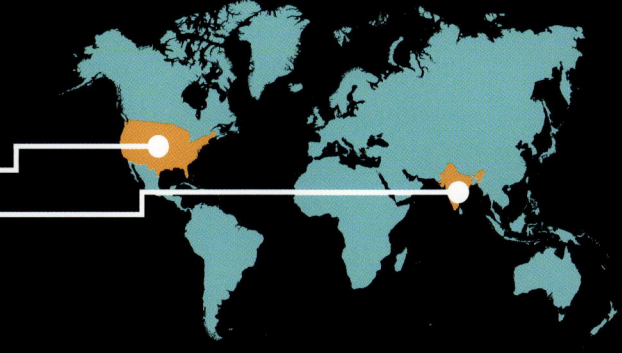

Bugs

When the code is not written properly, it can cause a problem with the program. This is called a bug. When programmers fix bugs, it is called debugging.

In 1947, a real bug was found in a calculator at Harvard University, in the US, which stopped the computer from working. However, mistakes in code were called bugs before this.

11

Smartphones

Mobile phones used to be much simpler machines that mainly made phone calls and messaged people (although sometimes they had games on them). However, now most phones are smartphones – this means they are like a phone and a computer combined together.

Features of a Modern Smartphone

Phone
Internet
Messages
Games
Maps
News
Camera
Music
Voice-Activated Assistant

There are around 2.6 billion smartphones being used in the world. 1 in 10 smartphones are sold in India.

A smartphone today is more powerful than the computers that NASA used to fly people to the Moon in the 1960s.

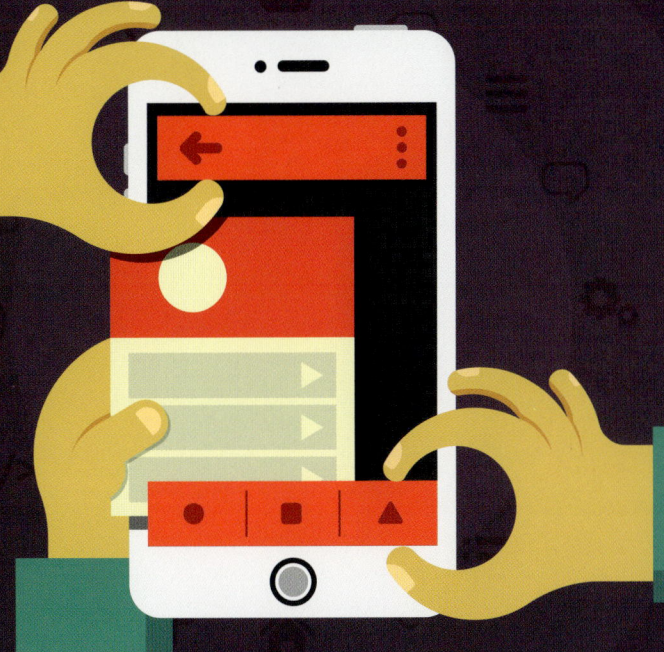

Most smartphones have one of two different operating systems – either Android or iOS. An operating system is the basic software that comes with a computer which helps it run. Android and iOS smartphones both have their own apps which can also be installed onto the phone.

As of 2017, there were around 2.2 million apps available for iOS, and 2.7 million for Android.

By 2020, the iOS app store is expected to have around five million apps. More and more apps are being created than ever before.

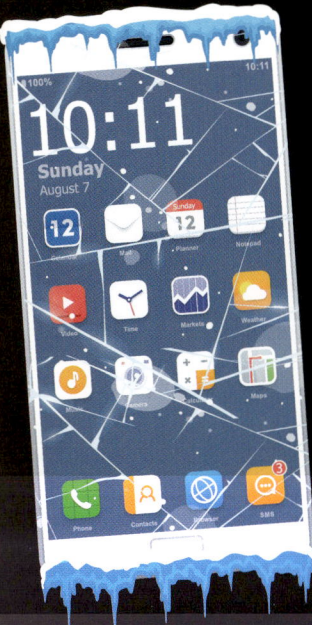

A colder smartphone runs out of battery faster. Apple, the company behind iOS, recommends that phones are always kept at a temperature above 0°C if possible.

The most expensive phone in the world is the black diamond iPhone. It is worth $15.3 million. It is fully coated with black diamonds. For that money, you could buy a brand new personal jet plane.

The Internet

The internet is the worldwide network which connects computers together. In 1969, the internet was invented by the US military. It became extremely popular in the 1990s after Tim Berners-Lee invented the World Wide Web, a type of software which makes it easier to share information and look at all the webpages on the internet.

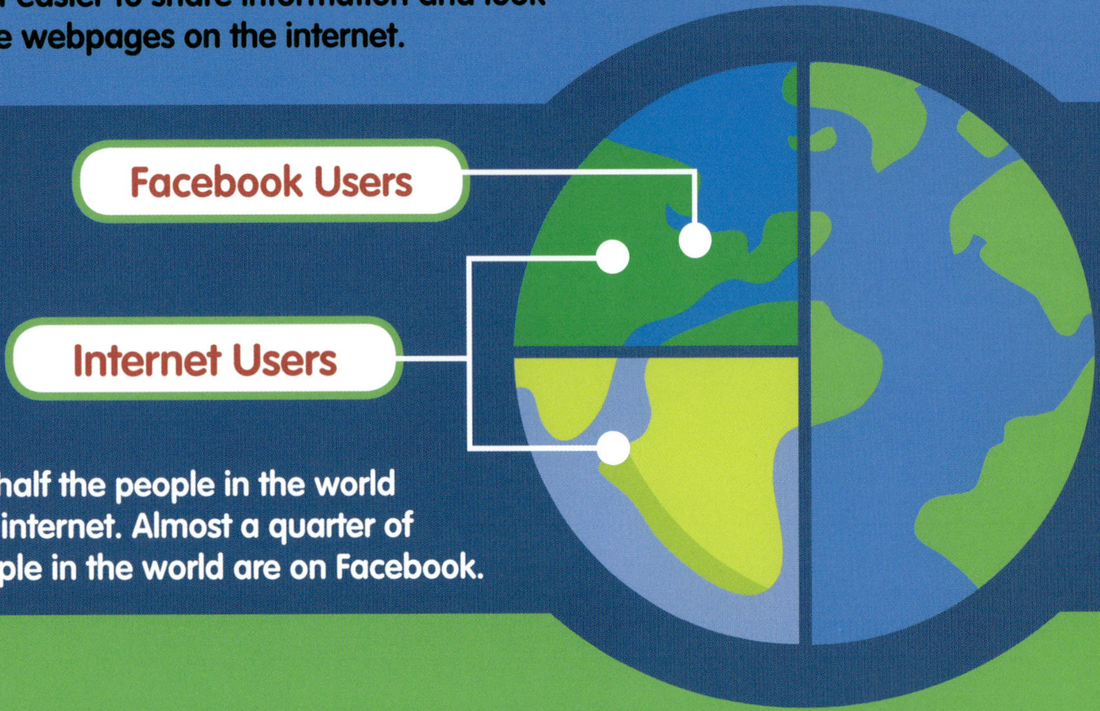

Facebook Users

Internet Users

Almost half the people in the world use the internet. Almost a quarter of the people in the world are on Facebook.

Around 3 million emails are sent every second. This is over 210 billion emails a day.

1.7 billion internet users are in China and India. Most of these are younger people.

Websites have endings such as '.com' or '.org'. These are called domain name extensions. Websites from different countries can have different domain name extensions – for example, '.co.uk' is for the UK, '.cn' for China or '.nz' for New Zealand. The most popular domain name extension is '.com'. There are over 123 million registered '.com' websites on the internet.

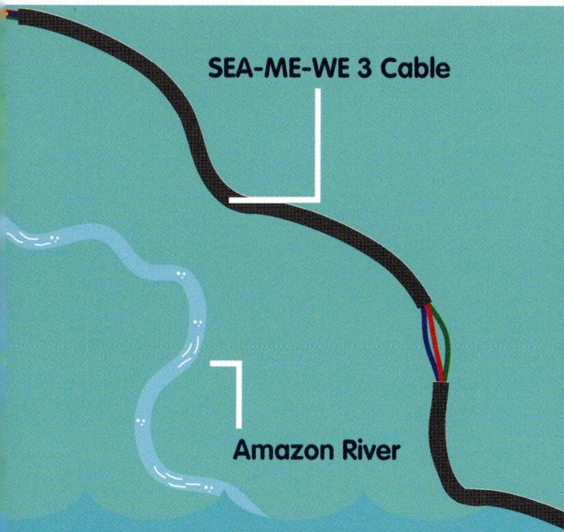

Down Where it's Wetter...

Cables and wires are used to connect different countries together over the internet. Some of these cables and wires travel along the bottom of the sea. The longest undersea internet cable in the world is SEA-ME-WE 3, which runs between Europe and Australia. It is 39,000 kilometres (km) long. That is more than five times longer than the longest river in the world, the Amazon River.

Internet cables at the bottom of the sea can sometimes be bitten by sharks. Google now protects its cables with shark-proof wrappers.

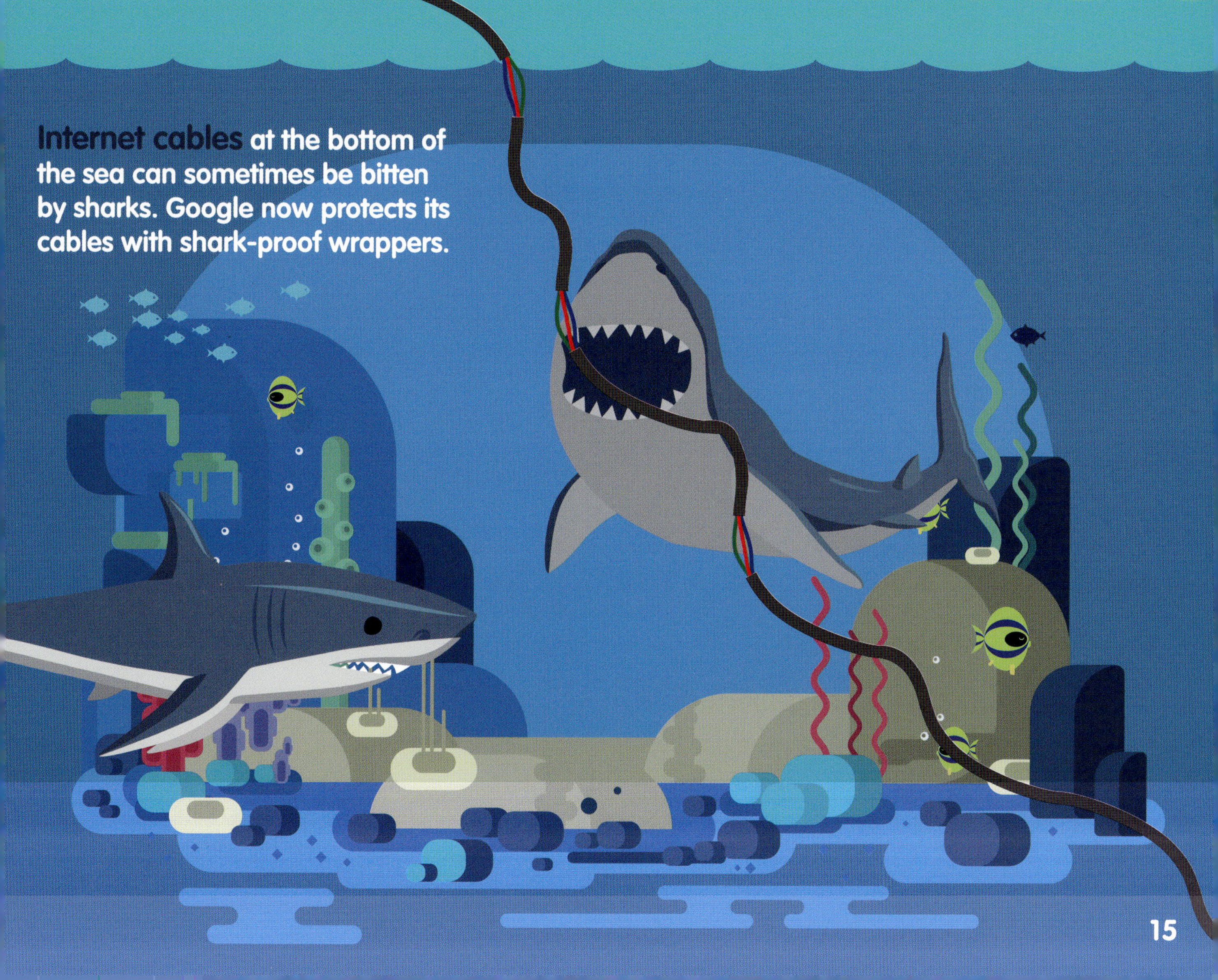

Computers in Everything

Our devices and technology are becoming more connected. Soon, all our devices will be able to talk to each other, in order to become smarter and more helpful. This is called 'The Internet of Things' because all of the devices would be connected, just like computers are connected over the internet.

Fridge of the Future

In the future, your fridge may be fitted with technology so it knows what is in the fridge. When the fridge runs out of something, like pizza, the fridge would be able to talk to another device, such as a laptop or desktop, and tell it to order more pizza.

Since 2008, more objects have been connected to the Internet than people.

Wearable Technology

Wearable technology can be built into clothes, or worn on the body. These devices can help with all sorts of things such as measuring heart rate, tracking how much time has been spent exercising, and recording how we sleep.

In 2017, around 113 million pieces of wearable technology were sold. Experts believe that around 222 million pieces of wearable technology will be sold in 2021.

2017　　　　　　　　　　　　2021

Self-Driving Cars

Self-driving cars have already been invented. The self-driving cars made by Google have driven over 3.2 million km, and have only had one accident.

Self-driving cars might be much safer than human-driven cars in the future.

Self-driving cars could also become part of 'The Internet of Things' when cars communicate with each other. This would help cars avoid each other, and also let them share information of any other problems on the road.

17

Rise of the Computers

Computers are becoming a bigger part of our lives every day. A lot of things that used to exist are now replaced by robots or digital computers.

Going Digital

Many people now talk to each other using digital technology.

This is usually through social media

Facebook and Whatsapp carry 60 billion messages between people every single day.

People across the world are also able to talk to each other face-to-face using video calls. This can help people who live far away to see their family or go to work using digital technology, instead of actually being there.

In 2010, 87 billion minutes of video calls were made over Skype.

92% of the world's money is digital. This means the money being transferred is counted on a computer, rather than being handed over in notes and bills for people to count.

In fact, most things are not paid for with coins or paper money any more. In many parts of the world, including the UK, more than half of all payments were made digitally, with a card.

Rise of the Robots

Robots that use computers are also becoming better at helping us in our everyday lives. Some people think that, in the future, robots will do lots of jobs that humans do now. This will give humans time to do other things that they are more interested in.

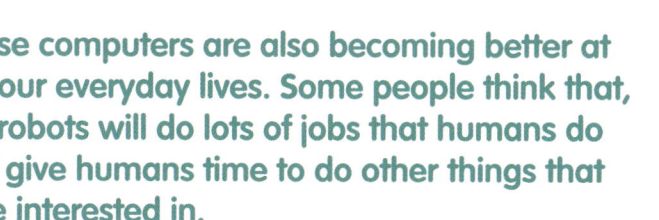

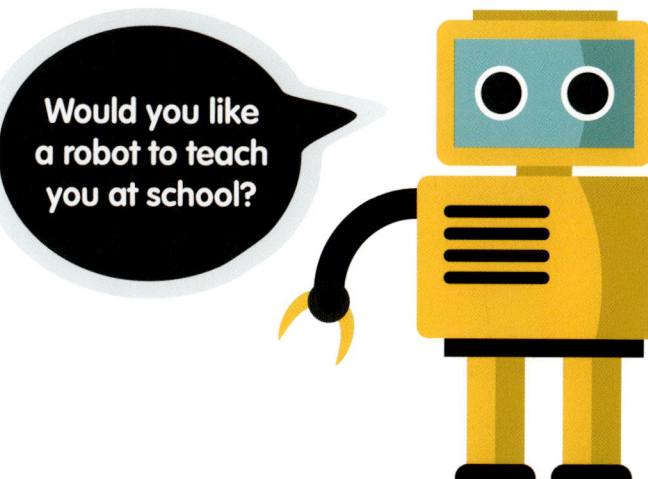

Would you like a robot to teach you at school?

Pepper and Nao

Pepper and Nao are two robots that were tested in schools in Singapore. They helped the teacher teach children about all sorts of things, from recycling to emotional skills.

Robots are getting better at all sorts of things, including talking to humans, running and jumping, and simple, repetitive tasks.

Boston Dynamics, a company that used to be owned by Google, creates robots that are especially good at moving around. Some of their robots can open doors and run 46 kilometres per hour (kph), while others can climb 35° slopes. The robots can walk through snow and mud, and can get back up after being knocked over.

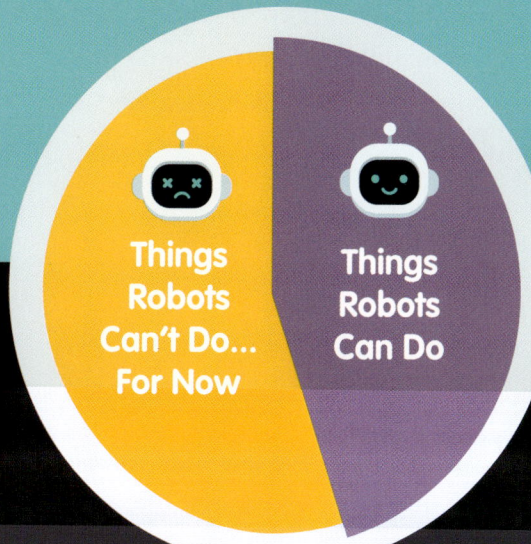

Things Robots Can't Do... For Now

Things Robots Can Do

Some organisations think that **45%** of activities that humans are paid to do could be done by robots instead.

19

Smaller Stuff

Computers have been getting smaller and smaller. The first computers that were invented were giant machines that would fill a whole room. Now we have computers that can fit into our pockets.

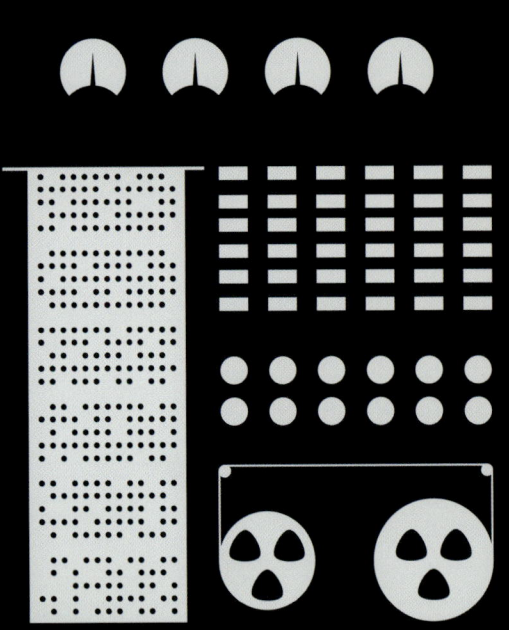

ENIAC was one of the first computers, and was built in 1946. It took up a whole basement and weighed around 27,215 kilograms (kg). That is more than four elephants.

The iPhone 7 Plus weighs around 188 grams (g). This means that the ENIAC weighed as much as 144,760 iPhones. However, any one of those iPhones would be more powerful on its own than the ENIAC computer of 1946.

The smallest computer currently in the world was created by IBM. It is 1 millimetre (mm) high and 1 mm long. This is smaller than a grain of coarse salt.

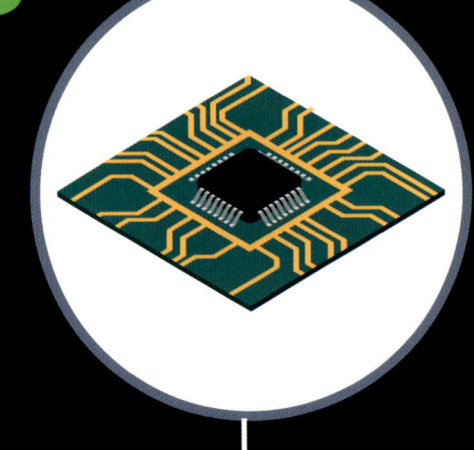

Moore's Law

In 1965, Gordon Moore noted that the number of components in a microchip was doubling every year. Moore's Law was then created, which is a prediction that every two years, microchips will have double the components and double the power. Until now at least, this has stayed true.

Tiny Transistors

Modern microchips can be around the size of a fingernail. They can have as many as two billion transistors each. The transistors are so small, a microscope is needed to see them.

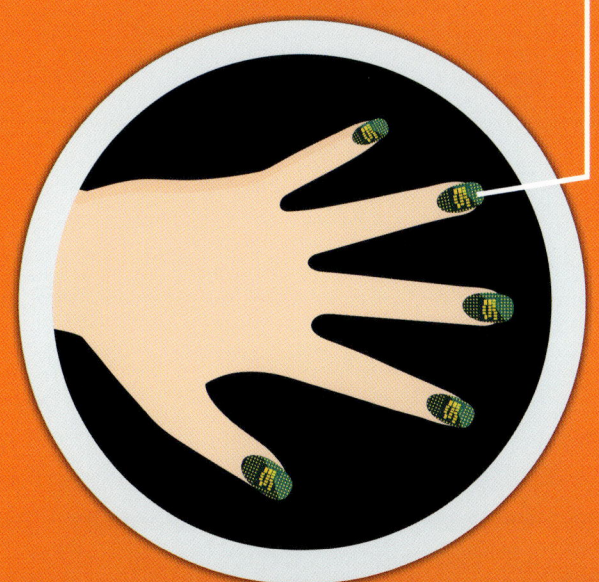

In a microchip, transistors can be 14 nanometres apart. Some experts think that the transistors will be only five nanometres apart in the 2020s.

The distances between the components that make up today's microchips are measured in nanometres. There are a billion nanometres in a metre. A human hair is around 75,000 nanometres thick.

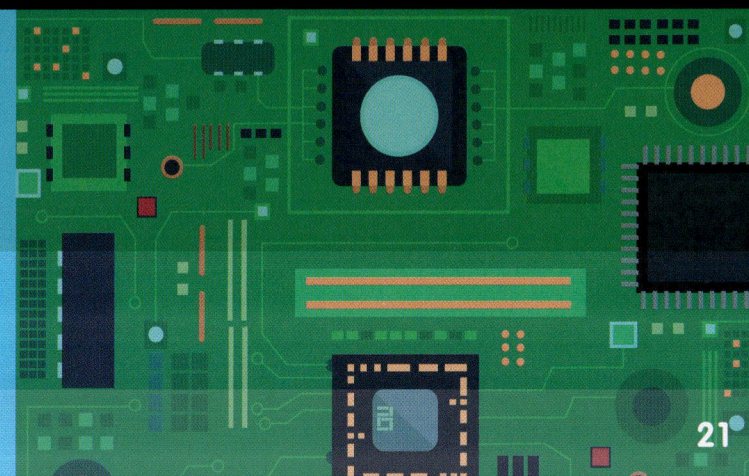

AI

Artificial intelligence, or AI, is a type of computer that can do more than just follow instructions. AI would be able to learn from its mistakes, have conversations and 'think' for itself.

Nobody has created a true AI yet, although many lesser types of AI exist.

Alan Turing was a scientist who did a lot of work into AI. He created the Turing test, which is a test given to a robot to see if it can <u>convince</u> other people into thinking that it is a human.

Google Assistant answered 60% of questions correctly.

Personalised assistants found in smartphones, like Siri or Google's Assistant, are not true AI. They use a lot of responses which have been programmed by a human. However, they are still intelligent. When asked 5,000 random questions, Google Assistant understood and answered around 3,000 correctly.

There is more AI around us than we think. 33% of people think they use AI technology. However, it is actually 77% of people who are using AI technology.

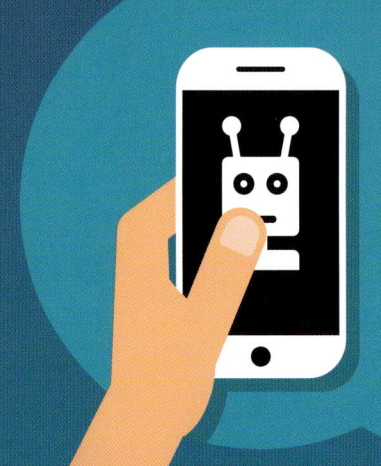

Man Vs. Machine

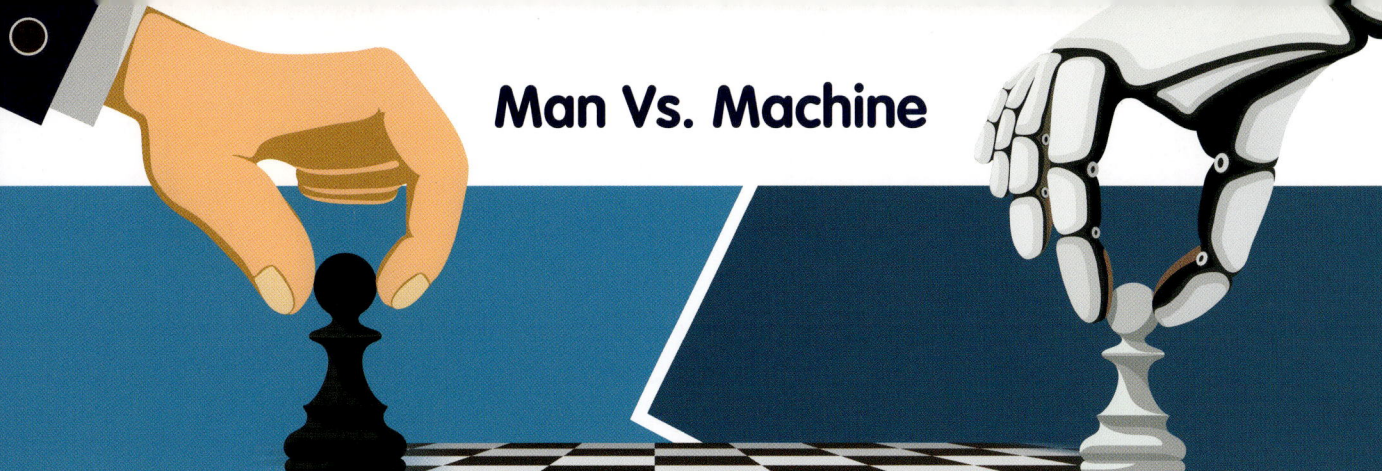

In 1997, AI won a game of chess against the world champion, Garry Kasparov. In 2016, AI beat the world's best Go player, Lee Sedol. Both chess and Go are complex board games, with many possible moves and lots of choices. Over the years, people thought that only humans could play these games, but AI has now proved them wrong.

AI is getting good at writing. One AI bot wrote over 1.5 billion pieces of writing in 2015. It may already be difficult to tell whether the books you read are written by humans or robots.

The human brain has around 86 billion neurons, many of them firing information around the body all the time. Some people think AI will never be as good at learning and problem solving as a brain.

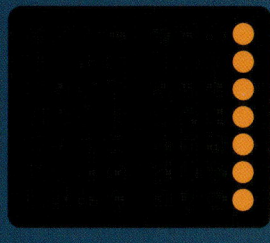

It took one of the world's most powerful supercomputers 40 minutes to calculate one second of human brain activity.

Inventing AI would create a lot of questions. If an AI passed the Turing test, would we treat them like a person? Would it be wrong to make an AI work all day and tell it what to do? We wouldn't treat a person like that, and some people think it would be wrong to treat a true AI like that.

Some people think AI could be dangerous. People like Stephen Hawking – a famous scientist – and Bill Gates – who owns Microsoft – have said that AI could take over the world from humans, or even harm us.

An AI might do this accidentally – in trying to save the environment for us, the AI might order machines to destroy all cars, cities and factories. Nobody knows how an AI would think.

AI might also answer all the world's questions. It might allow us to build even bigger and more powerful technology that help us do amazing things, like explore space or save the environment.

Extreme Computers

Water

In 1936, a Russian scientist called Vladimir Lukyanov built a computer that ran on water. To give the computer instructions, Lukyanov would change different taps and plugs. The computer could then work out the answer to some mathematical equations, and would tell Lukyanov the answer by filling up tubes with different amounts of water.

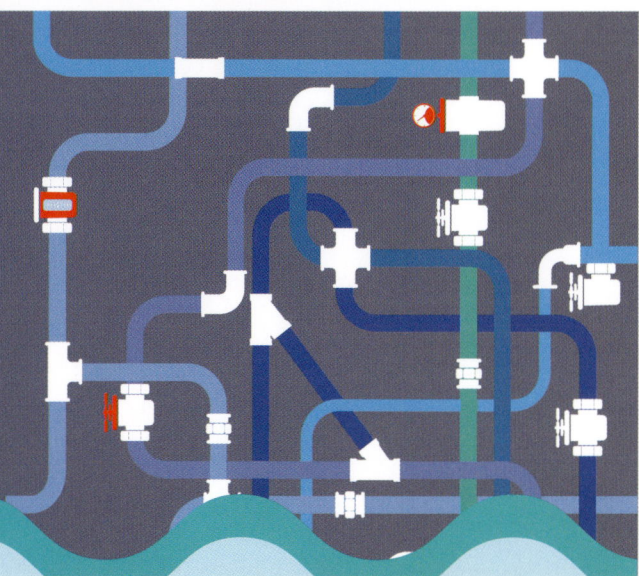

SAGE

The biggest computer system ever built was called SAGE. It was used to stop missiles attacking the US in the 1950s. It was a system of around 20 computers, and weighed 226,796 kg in total. That is a heavier than a blue whale.

Slime Mould

At the University of West England, scientists plan to make a computer that runs on slime mould. The slime mould is made up of tiny single-celled organisms which can travel around obstacles when looking for food. The scientists use the slime mould as circuits, and connect these circuits with normal electronic components. So far, the scientists have successfully experimented with the slime mould, and this might be the building blocks which lead to a type of slime-computer.

Supercomputers

Meet the Supercomputers

Supercomputers are giant, expensive computers that are extremely powerful. They are usually owned by an organisation or a government, and they carry out important or specific jobs that normal computers cannot do. Here are a list of some of the top supercomputers, and what they've got up to.

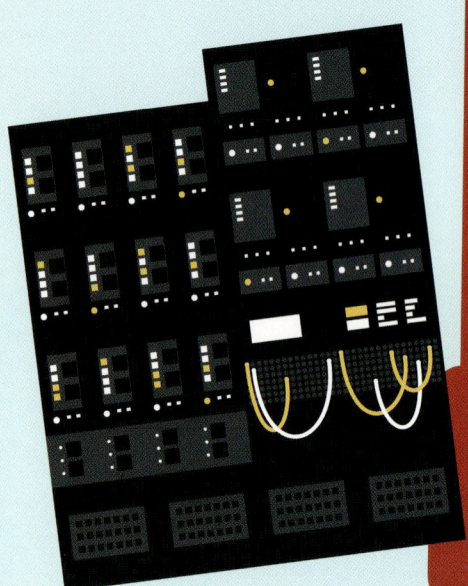

Fact File:

Name:
Cray XC40

Where:
Britain

Day Job:
Predicting the Weather – Cray XC40 is the most powerful computer in the world which is working on weather and climate.

Power:
Can do up to 14 trillion calculations per second.

Memory:
Has enough memory to hold 200 trillion numbers. Also has 24 petabytes of storage. This is enough to store 100 years' worth of HD films.

Fun Fact:
Cray XC40 takes in 215 billion weather observations, and uses these to guess what the weather will do next.

Fact File:

Name:
IBM Roadrunner

Where:
New Mexico, United States of America

Day Job:
Finding out when nuclear weapons would decay.

Power:
1 million billion calculations per second.

Memory:
103.6 terabytes

Fun Fact:
Even though it was one of the fastest computers in the world, the IBM Roadrunner was shut down after five years because it needed too much power to run. It needed 2,345 kilowatts an hour to do its calculations. Other supercomputers were invented which needed half the amount of kilowatts, and were just as powerful.

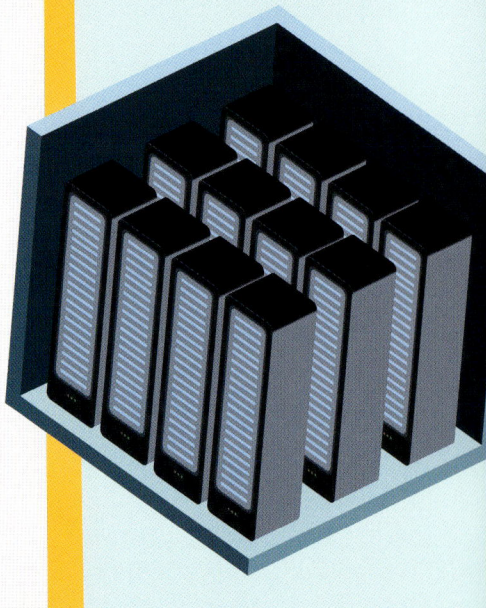

26

Fact File:

Name:
Blue Horizon

Where:
San Diego,
United States of America

Day Job:
Research for Universities.

Power:
1.7 trillion calculations per second.

Memory:
576 gigabytes

Fun Fact:
In around three billion years, our galaxy, The Milky Way, will crash into another galaxy, the Andromeda Galaxy.
To find out what would happen, Blue Horizon ran some calculations and tests, and worked out exactly how that would happen.

Fact File:

Name:
Blue Gene

Where:
California,
United States of America

Day Job:
Helping scientists see tiny things in the human body, and find out how they work.

Power:
280 trillion calculations per second.

Fun Fact:
It would take a scientist 177,000 years to perform all the calculations that Blue Gene does in a second.

Fact File:

Name:
Watson

Where:
United States of America

Day Job:
Watson is very powerful. Its job is to answer questions and solve problems. Watson works in medicine, figuring out why people are ill, and diagnosing serious diseases like cancer and ALS.

Power:
More than a trillion calculations per second.

Fun Fact:
Watson appeared on a TV show called Jeopardy, and won against the top two human contestants.

27

Future Devices

In the future, computers may look quite different. The devices we use are always changing. Here are a few types of computer devices that we may be using in the future.

Smart watches have already been invented, but they may become more popular in the future. Because they are on your body, they may be able to show all sorts of information such as heartbeat, as well as make phone calls and message people.

Google Glass was first invented in 2012. It had a camera, microphone and computer inside, which let people look at videos, words and pictures without needing a screen.

This means that people could search for things on Google or look up information on the move. Smart glasses like these may also become more widespread in the future.

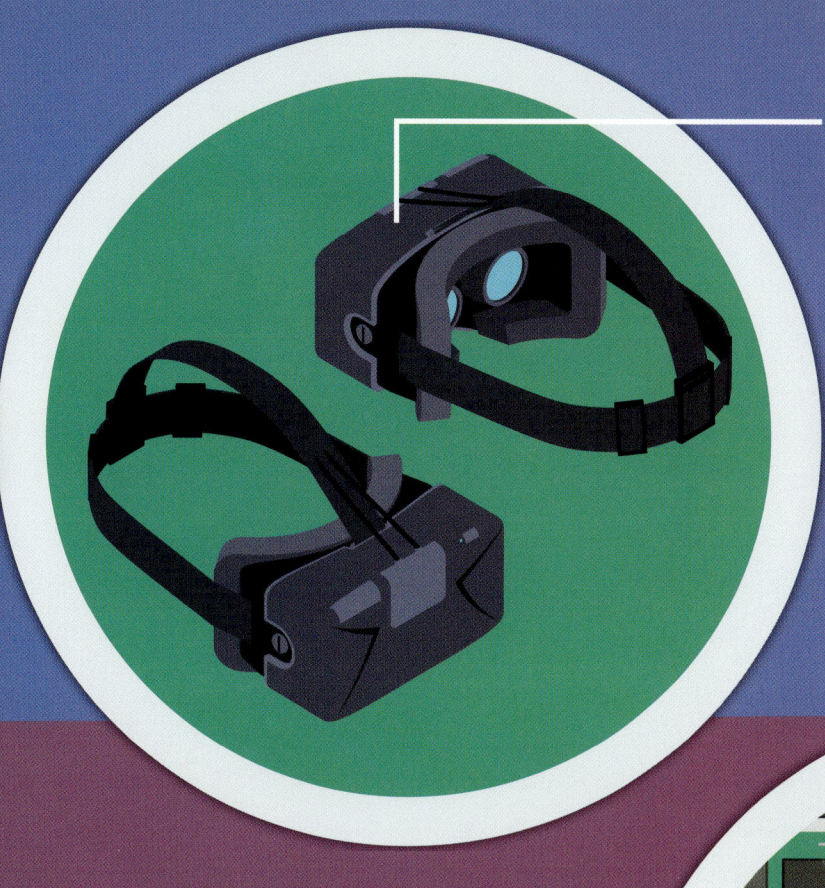

Virtual reality is becoming a big part of gaming, social media and watching videos. This device puts the person in the action, allowing them to look around and interact with their surroundings.

The person uses a headset and a pair of headphones to block out all light and sound, so they can only see and hear the virtual world. The virtual world can be anything, from outer space to the bottom of the sea.

At the moment, only 13 million PCs have the power to run virtual reality – that is less than 1% of the total amount of PCs. However, in the future, virtual reality will become cheaper and computers will become more powerful. This will mean more people will be able to use it.

Soon virtual reality might appear in schools and in homes all over the world. What would you do in a virtual reality?

Activity

Can you make a list of all the computers in the room you are in? What about the building? Don't forget all the hidden computers in things like toys and appliances.

If you had a supercomputer or an AI, what would you use it for? Talk about your ideas with your friends.

What do you think computers will be like in the future? Try drawing the different types of robots we might invent.

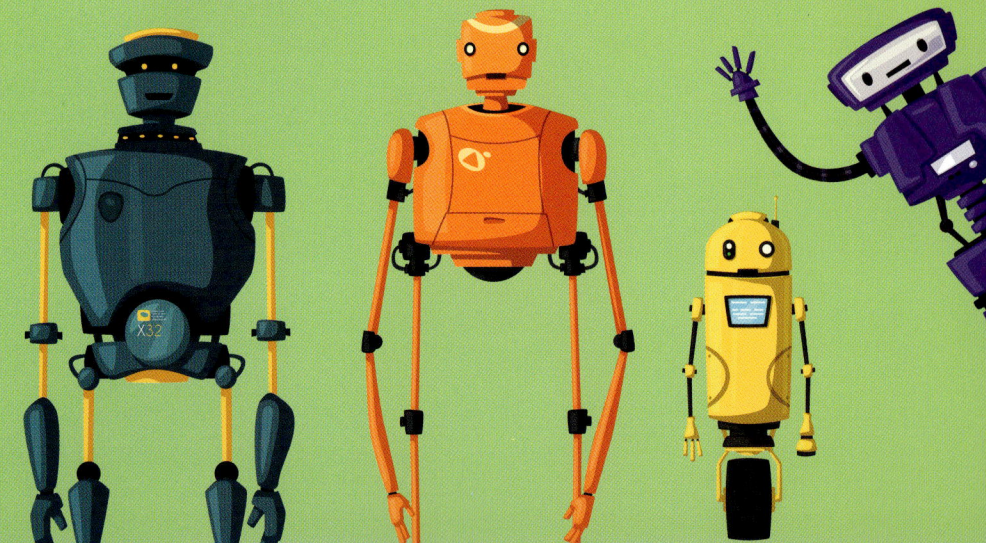

Glossary

ALS	a type of disease that affects control over voluntary muscles
billion	one thousand million
bot	a computer program that works by itself
calculate	to work something out, usually to do with mathematics and numbers
cancer	a serious disease caused by the uncontrolled dividing of cells
circuits	paths for electric current to move around
components	devices and other physical things that are connected to a circuit
convince	make someone believe something
decay	to rot or decompose
digital	information that is expressed as a series of the digits 0 and 1
emotional	in a way that relates to one's feelings and emotions
employed	paid to do work
equations	a type of mathematical sum which shows how two things are equal
estimated	guessed based on evidence
Go	a Chinese board game, one of the oldest in the world
information	facts about something
microchip	a very small piece of material in a computer full of circuits
NASA	the American space agency
neurons	cells in the body that carry information to and from the brain
nuclear weapons	very destructive weapons that use nuclear energy
observations	looking closely or making a note of something
physical	relating to the body
registered	recorded or listed
repetitive	happening again and again
signals	a sign or action which shows information or instructions
single-celled organisms	a very simple living thing made up of one cell, like germs or some types of algae
surroundings	the things and conditions around a person or thing
technology	machines or devices that are made using scientific knowledge
virtual	something that exists in computer software, rather than in the real world

Index

binary 6–7, 10
body 17, 23, 27–28
bugs 11
calculations 7, 23, 26–27
code 7, 10–11
components 8–9, 21, 25
desktop 4, 8, 16
digital 6–7, 18
email 7, 14
fast 11, 13, 26
future 5, 16–17, 19, 28–30
Google 9, 11, 15
hard drives 9
history 7
humans 10, 17, 19, 21–24, 27
instructions 4, 6, 10, 22, 25
internet 10, 12, 14–17
jobs 10, 19, 26–27

keyboard 4, 6, 8
laptop 4, 16
learning 5, 10, 22–23
memory 8–9, 26–27
message 12, 28
microchip 6, 21
microphone 28
money 13, 18
mouse 4, 8
phone 4, 7, 12–13, 20, 22, 28
powerful 4, 8, 12, 20, 23–24, 26–27, 29
problem-solving 6, 23, 27
program 10–11
programmer 10–11
robots 18–19, 22–23, 30
school 5, 19, 29
scientists 22, 24–25, 27
self-driving cars 17
smart 4–5, 7, 12–13, 16, 22, 28
social media 29
transistors 6–7, 21
virtual reality 29